BERTH

First published in 2012
by Bradshaw Books
Tigh Filí, Civic Trust House, 50 Pope's Quay, Cork
www.bradshawbooks.com

© Natalie Scott 2012
www.nataliescott.co.uk

ISBN: 978-1-905374-27-4

10 9 8 7 6 5 4 3 2 1

Cover Design and Typesetting by Twibill Design, Cork.

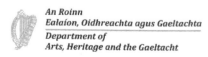

An Roinn
Ealaíon, Oidhreachta agus Gaeltachta
Department of
Arts, Heritage and the Gaeltacht

BERTH

VOICES OF THE TITANIC

natalie scott

bradshaw books

For the passengers and crew, their families
and Titanic, on the centenary of her death
2.20 am 15th April 1912

Acknowledgements

With special thanks to Howard Nelson of the Titanic Heritage Trust for believing in this project.

My gratitude also to Máire Bradshaw, Jamie O'Connell and Emer Duane of Bradshaw Books, David Edwards of Vivid Theatre Company, Annabel Turpin of Stockton Arc, and the Arts Council England for supporting the stage production of BERTH.

I'm indebted to the following people (listed alphabetically) for their support and encouragement throughout this project:

Lucy Adlington, David Almond, Neil Astley, Josephine Austin, Fred Bingham, Kath Bingham, Sylvaine Bowler, Jo Briggs, John Clarke, Carol Coates, Emma Conally-Barklem, Kath Conally, Garry Craig, Laura Degnan, Sara Dennis, Scott Dinning, Amy Featherstone, Helen Ferguson, David Fillis, Terry Gifford, David Gill, Claire Greaves, Annabel Grey, Robert Grierson, Gordon Hodgeon, Ross Johnson, Helen Kirk, Pauline Kirk, Jessie Lendennie, Marilynn Longstaff, Gill McEvoy, Jenny McKenna, Claire Malcolm, Jean Mead, Stephen Mills, Neville Moore, Blake Morrison, Rob Myers, Helena Nelson, Mike Newton, John Norman, John Norton, Jean O'Brien, Ré Ó Laighléis, Emily Owen, Sheila and John Pattison, Jadzia Race, Kerry Robson, Dorothy Scott, Nick Scott, Michael Shannon (BBC Northern Ireland), Christine Southwood, Joy Smith, Cathryn Summerhayes, Mandy Sutter, Brian Thurlbeck, John Tyson- Capper, Les Verrill, Rob Watson, Marianne

Wheelaghan, Janine Williams, Anna Woodford, and all of my wonderful English and Creative Writing students.

Special thanks to Tracey Iceton for being a great friend and mentor throughout this process and my father Tony Scott – honorary agent.

Finally, as always, thank you Pete.

Author's Note

Titanic has been there, somewhere in my waters for many years now; the ship who had to her name so much added weight and potential for greatness but is perhaps most universally famous for sinking. I realised early on that she had so much more to give. Her creation and journey have a wide appeal that begs you to compare your life to hers and, as you delve deeper, those she carried.

My research for *Berth* began with a fascination for the sea and the sheer opulence of the ocean steam liners that broke its surface. Built for speed, efficiency and luxury but most of all for an unabashed display of power, that of humankind over nature. Titanic and her passengers fell victim to this arrogance in a way comparable with the First World War and 9/11, and the Edwardians were forced to tend the wounding thought that nothing built by human hand is indestructible, least of all by nature itself. The disaster was a tragedy of over-confidence, poor decision-making and painful coincidence; historically documented details paint an almost unimaginable picture of failure but, once we've attempted to take stock of the horrendous loss of life, it is the personal accounts that really touch heart and mind.

This is how *Berth* was born; though extensively researched, it intends not to be solely a factual account of Titanic's life and death but a voiced exploration of the what-ifs, ironies, humour and hearsay, as well as the painful truths, presented from the imagined perspective of those directly and indirectly linked to the disaster. The aim ultimately is to mourn the dreadful losses whilst also celebrating the saved, through voices that are not afraid to express their thoughts, past or present, living or dead.

Natalie Scott

Contents

James Dobbins

(Shipyard worker for Harland and Wolff, Belfast. During construction of ship - LOST)

I was with her through the build,
from the laying of keel plates
to the last bristles of paint.

I considered myself lucky
to be called for launch-day;
many poor surplus souls
went missing a day's pay.

I'd been freeing a support
from the shores just below
her hull, as she strained
on the workings like a feral
animal tethered to its post.

When the support was freed,
the shore pinned down my leg
and I must've fallen unconscious
as I've been in darkness ever since.

Please tell me, because I'm dying
to know – did she make a good,
safe passage to New York?

Anchor

(One of three made for Titanic - SAVED)

It took twenty horses
to lug me
through the shipyard
on the back of a cart
like a fifteen-and-a-half ton
pantomime dame.

My spitting image was weighed
on the other side of the bow:
two fat men in drag;
we felt as though no-one
could ever
bring us down.

Mrs Florence Ismay

(Wife of SAVED: Mr J Bruce Ismay,
Chairman of the White Star Line)

I would never tell him this of course
but I had a strange feeling about that ship.
You can call it a woman's intuition now
but then it would have been nagging.
On holiday with our children, while
he sampled the sumptuous delights
of his latest dreams and desires,
I felt a little overthrown
and, silly really,
somewhat
barren.

I would never admit this to anyone else
but I couldn't help feeling some sense
of relief when I cradled my broken
empty husk of a husband
in my arms like my
first-born
son.

Store-Room

(G deck, aft - LOST)

Sweetbreads	1,000
Hothouse grapes	1,000 lb
Fresh asparagus	800 bundles
Spirits	850 bottles
First Class men lost	115 souls
First Class women lost	4 souls
Fresh meat	75,000 lb
Fresh fish	11,000 lb
Fresh cream	1,200 qt
Wines	1,500 bottles
Second Class men lost	147 souls
Second Class women lost	15 souls
Flour	200 barrels
Potatoes	40 tons
Sausages	2,500 lb
Beer and Stout	20,000 bottles
Third Class men lost	399 souls
Third Class women lost	81 souls
Ice cream	1,750 qt
Fresh milk	1,500 gals
Sugar	10,000 lb
Jams and Marmalade	1,120 lb

First Class children lost	1 soul
Second Class children lost	0 souls
Third Class children lost	53 souls

Jenny

(Cat - disembarked at Southampton before Titanic set sail)

All ships have a cat.
Folks say it's bad luck.
Best you make your own mind up.
We keep down the rats
- simple as that.

Luck had nothing to do
with what happened.
I felt it coming, like my waters
breaking.

The ship had a smell about it
and I kept seeing faces
floating fixed in the water.

That's why we left before she set
sail, me and my little chets,
no more than the size of rats
themselves.

The manoeuvre required care:
I took each in turn by the scruff
and paddled tentatively
across the gangplank.

My back was stiff
but I felt a weight
lift when all paws
touched dry land.

Mr Lawrence Beesley

(Second Class passenger - SAVED)

As I crossed Canute Road
her funnels grew like giant
candy sticks out of the office
rooftops, dwarfed still by her masts
reaching up to meet the clouds.

I curved my way along the dockside,
dodging the crowds, and watched
her enormous stern loom further
and further over my head
as I approached her side.

She had a defiance about her,
with that sheer bulk of rump,
almost saying 'I'm here; like it or lump
it'. She looked as if she may jump
out of the water at any moment.

Then I got a tingle of goose pimples
from head to foot:
'Wow! Are we really going on that?'

Mrs Alma Pålsson

(Third Class passenger - LOST)

I had the jitters as I got on the ship.

The thought of such a long trip
and setting up house somewhere new,
was exciting and scary at the same time.

We were herded into a tiny gangway,
then through a thick steel entrance
and had our eyes, tongues and hair checked
rather rashly by the doctor.

A maze of passageways greeted us
and we were hurried along by fraught
stewards, jabbing towards our cabins.

Echoes of babies' cries and confused calls
in foreign voices haunted the walls.
We were basically left to amble around
and eventually find our way.

Our berths were pretty comfy;
(a lot nicer than home in fact!)
- we even had our own wash basin,
so clean you could see your face in it!

But that new smell was everywhere
and I felt quite sick by it at times,
missing those so familiar ones of home.

Mrs Hudson J C Allison

(First Class passenger - LOST)

I was feeling anxious as I stepped aboard.

I have sailed many times but not
in such prestigious company.
I was worried I had packed unsuitable
outfits in which to meet the Astors.

We had arrived on our own boat train,
amidst flocks of hollering reporters,
and I felt so important, if a little unworthy.

We walked steadily up a sloped gangway
and were greeted by Chief Steward Latimer,
who was extremely courteous and so
pleasant with the children.

Having checked our ticket,
he escorted us over a plush blue carpet
to our staterooms.

The facilities were pleasing,
(if lacking the comforts of home)
but we did have a private bathroom
and the sheets were crisp and clean.

But everything smelled so new
and unfamiliar that I was helpless
to stop feeling homesick.

Bertram Slade

*(Brother to Tom and Alfred - all three were Firemen
assigned to Titanic)*

We'd been in 'The Grapes',
you know it, on Oxford Street,
for a quick one. It was different
back then; you didn't have your thick
carpet, purple paint and coffee cups,
or, come to think of it, *blimey,*
- that picture of the ship on the wall!

She was just a job to us all,
or that's what we told ourselves;
one we had to get tanked up for,
like anyone.

We put a few more away,
rasped a few jokes out, at the expense
of the bosses. The ale was warm
and tinny but helped to numb the senses
and we had a rough eye on the time.

We spilled out onto the street at ten to twelve
but, you know when the fresh air hits you?
We were *anyone's* – aye, aye sailor!
We aped down the road;
if you'd seen us, you would've called us
Neanderthals, numpties, nonces?
We rounded the corner of 'South Western',
nearly onto the dock but had to stop

for a train, light from its load of toffs,
chuntering away out of town,
blocking our way to the ship.

She was calling us like a mistress
to a pack of untamed dogs
and as she hitched her skirts
and steamed away, bang on twelve,
we went from privileged crew
to jobless gawpers, cursing that train
and the track it railed on,
for royally ruining our lives.

Mr John Pierpont Morgan

(Founding Owner of the International Mercantile Marine Company - did not sail on Titanic)

How can it possibly fail?
My empire is built on
steel.
Nothing can rock its foundations.
White Star Line is the
keystone
in its construction.

My pockets go deep;
take a dive, like Teddy did.
Now the government owes me
big.
No ocean is too small; I will
monopolise
and devour them all.

I eat ships for breakfast.
Titanic is just a rather
sweet
aperitif for what will follow.
I will have to loosen
my belt from the
strain.

As the ship steams, I will sit
to eat
and watch red juices flow

as I carve my meat.
I will pat my belly and
belch
to a deal well done.

Mr and Mrs Marvin

(First Class passengers: Mrs Mary - SAVED, Mr Daniel - LOST)

Mr:	We'd been married just under three months;
Mrs:	the very first wedding to be cinematographed;
Mr:	we staged a second ceremony to capture it,
Mrs:	then honeymooned for five gorgeous weeks.
Mr:	When we stepped aboard the mighty Titanic,
Mrs:	the luxurious film star fantasy was preserved;
Mr:	everything was new and we had to try it all,
Mrs:	until we had unintentionally sullied the room:
Mr:	chipped a doorframe, broken a bone china cup,
Mrs:	splashed little water droplets on the mirror,
Mr:	lathered the soap till it frothed in its dish,
Mrs:	wetted all the sweet white cotton towels,
Mr:	stained the sheets practising rapture,
Mrs:	our limbs stretched out like butterfly wings.

Bad Omen Stoker

(LOST)

At Queenstown we dropped
anchor, two miles off Roche's
Point, so I went for a breather.
Climbed all the rungs to the top
of the aft funnel and poked my
head out for a lungful of Irish air.
Couldn't see much but sea and sky
but if I leant forward I could just
about make out the new wide-
eyed faces coming aboard, filling
the aft Third Class promenade.
As the wind died down, I caught
a bit of Erin's Lament, piping
its tears out over the waters,
then I scuffed my way back down
to the dark furnace of my work.
They said I was a bad omen;
a member of the 'black gang'
with face of soot, rising up
like a devil fresh out of hell.
But everyone was out of place
on that ship and if less time
had been taken on forcing
all of us into the right boxes,
like mail in the slots, she might
have stayed afloat. I am now
washed clean; my face, shiny

and pink. Bad omen indeed;
cover your mouth with your
hankie and keep walking, until
you reach a mirror and see
who's to blame for this.

Marconigram

3.50pm 14th April 1912 (RECEIVED)

(Telegrams cost 12s 6d for first ten words, then 9d for each subsequent word)

Proceed transaction
cheque posted Queenstown
receive remainder on arrival NY

Frederick Allen

(Lift Steward - LOST)

That sinking feeling was a part of my job. Up
and down through the length of my shift, peeling
away the layers of luxury with each deck descended.
A smooth ride, eavesdropping on whispered
conversations of new money gossip when they forgot
I was there. Listening to the rustle of silk skirts
and, while breathing in the heavy perfume,
imagining what it could be like underneath.

They didn't all smell so good, especially
after a rich dinner, the men taking my services
to the smoking room, shuffling as their bloated
bellies filled their suit trousers.
I made a few bob on tips from the more
appreciative passengers. Some even talked to me,
thinking I must be bored; inviting me up
onto the prom for a game of quoits, as a joke.

I was kept busy taking them to the boat deck.
But, as the panic set in, most took the stairs.
It didn't sink in with me until I pressed E deck
by mistake and a load of green water poured in.
Everything still worked – it didn't make any sense.
I decided I would do my bit until the lift stopped
working, thinking it never would and here I am still.
So, Madam, can I take you up?

Marconigram

6.05pm 14th April 1912 (LOST IN TRANSIT)

(Telegrams cost 12s 6d for first ten words, then 9d for each subsequent word)

Good crossing may arrive early
        much news carrying extra weight
                love you

Frederick Fleet

(Lookout in Crow's Nest - SAVED)

It was a night of threes and other odd numbers.
We were missing a set of glasses but the naked
eye's as good. One sea, like an oil slick pricked
with stars. No moon, no ripple. No swell.
Reggie's irregular breath in the cold.

Clouds formed odd shapes in front of our faces;
seeing things that weren't there. Threefold silence,
in bars, the rhythm of a waltz below:

One ... two, three...

One ... two, three...

One ...   black ...   mass

growing wide like a blind spot. Object directly ahead.
Three rings of the bell: 'Iceberg right ahead!'
Trapped in the carriage of a white knuckle ride,
we waited in watery-eyed silence:

'Turn...   turn...   turn'

cursing through our teeth,
my heart a tick-tocking
over-wound clock.
After triplets of seconds she swung to port
and we shaved a piece of ice as a souvenir.

'That were close.'

William McMaster Murdoch

(First Officer - LOST)

Hard over ... hard over!
Black ice buckles her starboard
side and I feel every shudder
haunt parts of me not
ready for failure.

This couldn't be my fate.
I had only ever done the right
thing: top honours at school;
sole representative of my siblings
at sea; sole representative
of *Titanic* in passing Board of Trade
first off ... check ... check ... check.
Faithful to White Star:
Fourth Officer on *Medic*,
Third, Second, First on *Titanic*
and should have been Chief
if not for Wilde ... check!

I intended to port around it, Sir.
Hard a' starboard, hard a' port.
I am not a man of mistakes
- check my records.
Order, order ...

There was no order that night.
No authority to take charge.
A house of cards breaking

like *Collapsible A*: Fill and lower!
Mine were full. No distinction
between child, woman, man,
second, first, third. I locked
eyes with theirs as they sparkled
and blurred into the sea,
wide and harried, their prayers
freezing white mist in the air.

Resignation caught the back
of my throat, making me boke,
like gulping brine. Those waters -
my wife, best friend, unborn bairns
reflected on the surface; my life.

You want to know if I did it –
murdered two then myself?
All I recall was an agony, hers,
slipping into numbness,
ringing ears, shots fired.
I saw myself from the stars,
so small and sinking fast
against a backdrop of such
grandeur, such expectation,
such responsibility ...

Hard over, I say ... hard over!
Those orders choke out
in a dull sob to the depths.
Hard over ... a' port ... hard over...

Mr Ernest James Crease

(Third Class passenger - LOST)

I'd been havin' a smoke
in our piece of deck up front,
when this huge crash came down
from nowhere, makin' me jump.

I stubbed my cigarette out
on one chunk and kicked
the other back. A few of us
started a game of football.

Even some of them up top
came down to join in - silly sods
were puttin' bits in their pockets
like they'd never seen ice before,

waddlin' in their penguin suits
like they'd wet themselves.
I nearly split me shirt buttons
from laughin' so much.

Rigel

(Black Newfoundland Dog - SAVED)

As the big float went through water
the warm meat juices made two
shoelaces of spit trail my jowls.
I remember smells and a word:

Clean slippery walkies path;
not enough dirt yet from people
in high collars with their little yappers
clicking along faster than me.

Heavy flower headache smell
from a high-pitched hand
needing warmth before going
into the shiny black.

Fear in the clouds coming out
of their mouths, open wide
but not for food. My master's smell
gone, 'hard over!' Gone? ... yes, gone.

(Thought it a game at first; so many
sticks to fetch, but the sticks got bigger
and the throwers were stiffening.
I paddled away to the bright.)

Sickly leafy smell on yellow tipped
fingers of hands dragging me up
the side of a new float:
one that smells of pain.

I learnt a new word that day:
God. Must be big, as they said it
a lot with good. Good God, good
God, blessing me backwards.

Mrs J Stuart White

(First Class passenger - SAVED)

When we struck ice I thought back
to my schooldays and bags of marbles
spilling across parquet floors.

The lifeboat was manned by schoolboy
stewards who didn't even know how
to row: 'Try putting it in the oarlock!'

Then one decided to light a pipe
in a boat full of woollen blankets!
How awfully ironic that the only able
bodies went down with the ship.

I'm sure I annoyed them all
when I hitched up my skirts
and took an oar, plunged it in
and showed them how it's done.

I'm sure they cringed at the sight
of me waving my walking cane
with electric light at Carpathia,
thinking: *mad old bitch; let's throw
her overboard and be well rid.*

And I wanted that bag of marbles,
just to split open into the bottom
of the boat and watch them peck

over the brightest ones,
while their livelihoods and reputations
divided beneath them on the ocean bed.

Miss Helen Lorraine Allison

(First Class passenger - LOST)

Mommy said we go boat ride.
I wanted look fishes to see
if they fins all stiff like Daddy
said they be.

Mommy look excited.
She kept smile at me
like other ladies on deck, all smiling
and blowing white clouds at me.
Some patted my head like sick doggy.

Mommy said 'look at the lights'.
Pretty colours on the sky made me
go 'wow' and I saw the ice Daddy
said was 'naughty berg' and I wanted
to know who lived there.

Mr Thomas Andrews

(Managing Director of Harland and Wolff Shipbuilders - LOST)

Rock-a-bye baby, in the tree top.
She's got twenty minutes to live
according to the mantelpiece clock
teetering forward on the brink
of suicide. I checked the time
by my pocket-watch this morning
at five past nine and it is correct
to the second. How many seconds?
A simple calculation: twenty by sixty
- twelve hundred seconds,
less ... two, less ... two.

When the wind blows, the cradle will rock.
I can still smell the varnish like it was brushed
on yesterday. That reminds me, I need
to put those orders through tomorrow
and the screws in the stateroom hat hooks
must be reduced and Mrs White's table lamp
bulb replaced. I have so much to organise,
arrange, discuss; notes to make and records
to keep. So why am I so calm?
My lifebelt rests full of death on the table.
Far too few boats for such a perfect ship.

When the bough breaks, the cradle will fall.
It's my sweat that beads up through her rivets,
my tears that rain down the lengths of her plates,
my blood seeping through the gash in her side.

There's dust on the painting that bears down
over my head. I run my finger along the groove
where frame meets image: a ship in Plymouth
Harbour, steaming happily ahead.
Another job for tomorrow.

Everything's at acute angles now.
I must look a picture propping up
the mantelpiece – chairs scrape
the floor - ashtrays spill their dust

as they smash the scattered
remains of one last Dutch courage
game of Bridge.

And down will come baby …
I want to hold everything in place,
screw them down, realign things,
build a cradle in the ocean
to rest her on.

Miss Mary Mangan

(Third Class passenger - LOST)

The priest was reciting
the rosary and I wanted
to join the others huddled
around him.

It was like walking
on a polished world
gone awry
and the wooden slope
was getting harder
to climb.

When a woman lost
her grip and started
to slide
down the deck
past me,

still clutching her rosary beads
and screaming for absolution,
as her skirts lifted
up and over
her head,

I wondered what sort
of God could choose
such a humiliating
exit from this
world.

John George Phillips

(Marconi Wireless Operator - LOST)

— · — ·   — — · —   — · ·

this can't actually be real

· · · — — — · · ·

trying to work 'Cape Race'

— · — ·   — — · —   — · ·

hundreds of messages to send

· · · — — — · · ·

haven't time for ice warnings

— · — ·   — — · —   — · ·

passengers will be complaining

· · · — — — · · ·

need to do my duty for Marconi

· · · — — — · · ·

she's thrown a propeller that's all

... — — — ...

... — — — ...

... — — — ...

... — — — ...

... — — — ...

... — — — ...

— . — . — — . — — .. CQD (International distress call)
... — — — ... SOS (newly recognised distress call
during Titanic's life)

Mr Thomas Leonard Theobald

(Third Class passenger - LOST)

Aye, the gates at the top of the stairs were locked
but we were not kept below decks.
Our cabins were flooded not long after we struck
and the ripple of engines had throbbed to a stop.

A steward in a fresh white coat stood
on the other side with a look
of sympathy on his face but I knew the devil
was in there somewhere, as I saw fire in his eyes.

They wouldn't budge – fuck that for a game of soldiers!
We sniffed out our way like the rats
they wanted us to be:
              wound
                     our way
       a l   stairs, slid
         on   i
         g   of   n
    c o r r i d o r s , up a set   t
                                              o   water - w
                                                          r
                                                        o
                                                        n
                       back again,   !y a w   g
       electricity   f   i   k   r   n
                  l   c   e   i   g,
           our voices   clamouring
through the dying ship.

Until the stairs **widened** and the carpet **THICKENED**.
A huge dome appeared over our heads
and a grand entrance leading to an even grander saloon,
with round tables and silver spoons.

Someone hollered and we stopped a minute,
taking in how the other half live. I thought,
if this is what it takes to get into first class
you can shove it right up your arse.

Mr Benjamin Guggenheim

(First Class passenger - LOST)

Had I known Titanic would actually sink,
I may have worn the lifebelt
handed to me so diligently by my valet.
No, I believed, at that moment, in money
keeping us afloat; you can't sink class!

I had my valet dress me for dinner
then himself, and we sat all decked-out
in the reception room, stiff with wealth,
brandy in hand, waiting for a man
to give us the all-clear.

All I thought, when water lapped
against my shoes, was of my need to ensure
the boot boy did a good job
in polishing the lustre back into them,
in time for tomorrow's luncheon.

We were *not* prepared to go down
as gentlemen. Like the ship, I was not built
to be sunk. I tipped my hat
to the steward and prepared
to get drunk.

Victor Giglio

(Valet to Mr Guggenheim - LOST)

Is it not amusing that through life
you remind me of our differences
in rank, with *me, my, mine,*
while I attend to your every need.

And yet in death '*we* are prepared
to go down as gentlemen', *we*
are in it together – united,
brothers, almost.

But there is no plural
- it's all quite singular:
wherever you go
I suppose I must follow.

Captain E J Smith

(Captain of R.M.S. Titanic - LOST)

What if we had been equipped with more lifeboats?

What if this was not her maiden voyage?

What if I had been on the bridge on impact?

What if we were not making twenty-two and a half knots?

What if we had carried fewer passengers on board?

What if only the first four compartments had flooded?

What if the boats had been filled to capacity?

What if we had ensured an extra pair of glasses was in the crow's nest?

What if I had posted up the *Amerika's* ice warning in the chartroom?

What if we had carried out a passenger lifeboat drill?

What if we had not rebuffed the *Californian's* ice warning?

What if the waters were not freezing?

What if we had hit the berg head-on?

What if it had not been a crystal calm ocean?

What if the lifeboats had returned to pick up those in the water?

What if the *Californian* had responded to our CQD?

What if we had not nearly collided with the New York when leaving Southampton?

What if she had been a smaller, more manoeuvrable vessel?

What if there were not so many dignified guests on board?

What if that stoker's head had not appeared out of the funnel at Queenstown?

What if that cat with her litter of kittens had not been on board?

What if I had chosen roast duckling instead of fillet mignon for dinner?

What if I had retired last year?

What if I was not captain?

What if I was not captain?

Mrs Margaret JJ Brown

(First Class passenger - SAVED)

You can call me Maggie now we're friends.
Only artistic licence christened me Molly, long
after this old carcass here had fleshed the earth.

I was first class, or so the ticket said but my heart
would often be in steerage. It sinks even now when I think
of them sitting on their bunks, damp footed,
resigned to their lot.

Mine was a lottery: struck gold in JJ! A lucky break allowed
me to shine in the soup kitchens and the Press Club
- use what you've got girls! Count yourselves lucky
for your modern men. No one ever filled
my hot water bottle once a month.

Shouldn't joke about water. So cold it bruised me that night
and I wasn't submerged. I didn't wallow any more than when
I tried to make small talk with the Astors two hours earlier.
I got lucky again – always use your luck to help those
less fortunate. Common sense. Get on with it.

First Class got me a lifeboat seat. No point being a martyr
- you can't help people if you're dead. I wrapped my wealth
around many that night. Felt the weight lift from me as I tied
a sable stole feet to feet around a man's legs. I ordered them
to row, their heads hanging like wilted daisies.
Even Hitchens shut up.

I can take any man and why the hell not?
He would've taken me! It's lies about the revolver
though - I'm a strong woman, not a goddamn maniac.

The ship going down was shocking, yes,
but I'm a practical woman. I tend to look not back
but forwards to the future. Get rescued, stay alive
to save others. Bodies, hearts, minds. I couldn't get
the boat to go back so it had to be forwards.

With each strike of the oar a widow was made
and she didn't seem to care. I knew I would have
these pieces to pick up on board Carpathia
and then use my lace handkerchief to mop the tears
on dry land. That's what kept me going, I guess.

John R Jago Smith

(Postal Clerk - LOST)

Dear Mary,

I just wanted you to know
that my first thought,
when water came pouring
up into the sorting office,
was of you and how I never
send you letters.

I tried my best with the mail.
Did my duty to His Majesty, the ship
being a Royal Mail Steamer and all.
I was responsible for that mail.
Managed to haul some sacks up
the stairs. We just weren't equipped
for the speed of the sinking
and too many envelopes
floated transparent
with their messages
exposed.

But it was your face I saw,
as I went back down
for the last sack,
melting into the waters,
with the inky stains

of two hundred
'I love you's.

Yours always,

John.

Father Byles

(Second Class passenger - LOST)

I stood at the back
of the ship with my arms
outstretched over the railings
and they surged up from the depths
and over towards me with open faces
like I was their saviour and I thought
of how our Lord must have felt
when he turned water to wine at Cana:
the luminous mystery of the rosary.
'My hour has not yet come.'

We are all sinners and we will be absolved
in the eyes of God so that we are ready
to meet him in the Kingdom of Heaven.

This water washes us of our wicked deeds
and of our arrogance; we are once again
baptised in the name of the Father.

Violet Jessop

(Stewardess - SAVED)

Women on ships are in a kind of sea desert;
parched from obscuring their feminine charms
to avoid groping hands behind closed doors.

They mourn dried out relationships;
lost loves remembered in rusted passing ships,
blowing hot kisses towards the smell of land.

So, how strangely quenching it was
that upon my rescue I should be the one
amongst the shivering human shapes

with a forgotten baby cradled to my breast,
warming a tiny pair of feet as, by the minute,
each of my ship's illuminated lines went out.

Charles John Joughin

(Chief Baker - SAVED)

One more for the road.
Smuggled this scotch from kitchen
- a fine malt – ah, the mellow stuff,
sweet and sour, like all of this
- perfect drink to die by.

Just one more for the road.
Nothing to lose. She slides down
easily. Ha-ha! The glass won't
stay flat on the table, so I'll
hold it in my hand.

For the road – hurrah! – one more.
Sweet amber angel, wicked heart
of a temptress. I'll throw some
deckchairs overboard for those
poor drowning bastards.

One f'th road. One more.
She's going down hard. I'll give out bread
- shame to waste those fresh-baked
loaves, then I'll get to her stern
and cling on for as long as I can.

It's a-one f'road, jus'one.
I'll – ah, that's the spot!
Step into the sea as she goes
down and not even get
the top of my head wet!

Wone more an' none maw! Hey!
Bottle's nearly polished. H...hic!
I'll swim in the water for two hours,
sozzled, I won't feel the cold,
then get picked up.

Jush a'wone maw fuzee rowd.
... wone maw ...
    ... jussun .... ahhhh.

Mr Emil Richard

(Second Class passenger - LOST)

HELP! AIDEZ-MOI! HELP ME!
JE NE PEUX PAS NAGER.
CAN'T SWIM. I can't swim.
PLEASE. S'IL VOUS PLAIT.
PLEASE. please. Sauve
une seule vie. SAVE
ONE LIFE.
save me.

hel ... lp me ...
aide ... ne peux ... can't
plea ... vous ... please
sauve ... un ... save
one ... moi ...
seule
seu ...
s ...

Lady Duff-Gordon

(First Class passenger - SAVED)

You *will* have heard of me.
My good name often precedes me.

Oh, how I loved the polysyllabic
beating of our full names,

like coins exchanging hands,
when we were pronounced 'Man and wife'.

After dinner, I tweak each finger
of my lace gloves in time to the rhythm:

La-dy Lu-cy Chris-ti-an-a Duff-Gor-don
and watch them float down onto the bed.

Of course, I have my own fashion house.
I design personality dresses

of highest sophistication, for ladies of class;
a certain selection of je ne sais quoi

in lace and taffeta and silk: *Lucile* –
it epitomises elegance, *n'est-ce pas?*

Oh goodness, this noise is *insufferable*
- can we not move the boat further away?

Gosh, you *do* look a fright, dear –
your little dress is quite ruined

but don't worry, it looks cheap
and so is easily replaced.

There, there now
- all is *not* lost!

I'll give you some of my best styling tips,
just as soon as we are back onboard ship.

Miss Elizabeth Shutes

(First Class passenger (Governess) - SAVED)

Of course hindsight changes everything:
we did the same after *The Great War*,
that other paradox to sugar-coat the truth.
If they could have layered 'The Unsinkable Ship'
with marzipan and frosting they would have.
Anything made of iron can sink! You don't
have to be an engineer to know that.
We soon realise the painful ironies rising up
like air bubbles from tired lungs,
to belch out a laugh on the surface.

Nothing will ease the pain I feel in my mind
when I remember the icy waters boiling
with thrashing limbs; their noise at first
like hungry seagulls fighting over the last
flesh of fish, gradually becoming sedate,
some shrieking, some weeping, some
pleading gargled prayers to the stars,
forced to sit upright in their lifejackets.
When I looked hard, I caught a twinkle
of light in their eyes before I shut my own,
imagining them staring, glazed and lost
towards the rescue that would never come.

Unimaginable, *their* pain, I know how cold
I felt and, though dry, the air was dusting
a layer of frost over my hair and eyebrows.
Life and death in a deep pitted nutshell:
their agony, like losing a limb, we'll never tell.

Wallace Hartley

(Bandmaster - LOST)

One, two three; *one*, two three

I'm now at rest with my
palms up to hold close my
remembered violin
inscribed with 'for Wallace
on the occasion of
our engagement' from dear
wife to be, Maria.

She never recovered, never remarried

My time on Titanic,
hectic as always, with
show deadlines to meet in
First Class rooms, while diners
gorged on rich new flavours.
First time as quintet on
The White Star Line, we played all
company choice tunes plus
some requests: waltz, ragtime
upbeat and all that jazz.

Nearer my God to thee, Nearer to thee

Possibly. Quintet joined
trio and we worked hard
to keep them calm as she

went down hard by the head.
Octet of crying strings
singing into the dark
up to our waists in cold;
string fingers red raw with
exposure; bow knuckles
white as bone in their grip.

First time playing together and our last

You have my violin,
recovered ninety years
after I plunged to the
ultimate orchestra
pit, but do put your ear
to the skin of the sea:
forty one, forty six,
north fifty, fourteen west;
hear me play Autumn Waltz.

All eight of us perished, all eight of us play on

The Sage Family

(Third Class passengers - LOST)

Sage, Mrs Annie	44
Sage, Mr John George	44
Sage, Miss Stella	20
Sage, Mr George	19
Sage, Mr Douglas	18
Sage, Mr Frederick	16
Sage, Miss Dorothy	13
Sage, Master William	11
Sage, Miss Ada	9
Sage, Miss Constance	7
Sage, Master Thomas	4

Second Class Plate

(on Titanic - SAVED)

Before the ship set sail
I was unpacked from a box
and berthed at the bottom
of the stack on the dresser.
I was worried I would crack
from the pressure.

Each luncheon I would prepare
myself to be taken, as the weight
of those above me grew less,
to be filled with culinary delights
and scraped clean with silver
fork and knife:

my duty and purpose fulfilled;
the little blue and white china plate
with winding grapevine pattern
from Stonier & Co. Liverpool,
on reserve to serve those
in the middle.

Always a bridesmaid,
as she fell, down I went,
still stuck to the dresser;
locked in a glossy kiss
between glaze
and polished wood.

Now, years later, you handle me
with kid gloves, tarnish me
with your heavy breathing.
Just look at me; the only one
of my kind, preserved in a state
of plate virginity:

up on a plinth
to be wowed at
but never used.

Iceberg

(North-Atlantic Ocean - LOST)

It wasn't just
me there - there was
a whole pack of us. We were floating south
for the summer. If it hadn't been me, it would have been
one of them. I was a giant back then. They had their chance
to spot me – not difficult you'd think - I was no growler – well built
on top and packed a punch below the water line. They had their
warnings - should've known I'd be there. They said I ripped
a thirty foot gash in her side. They printed my frigid image
in The Times, pointing out a 'red smear' of paint on my
surface - a frantic smudge of lipstick (we left our
mark on each other!) They bent the truth as much
as I make a habit of bending steel. There was no
gash, just a buckling of metal and her stitches
popped. (An eye for an eye!) She took a piece
of me and her passengers played football
with it on the deck! I wore the red smear
for several months before I melted
down into the brine. It must have
remained for some time as
a red circle, like whale
blood, spiralling
into the
waters.

Mrs May

*(17th April 1912. York Street, Southampton. Husband and son -
LOST)*

That's last of the coal.
I 'ope news comes afore
it turns to ash in't grate.

This here's me youngest,
grinning 'er cherub chups away,
little devils of firelight in 'er eyes.

The food ha'n't run out yet but
there's eleven of us here. My eldest
only signed up bin the strikes

and 'is father should of been
on Britannic but 'is gammy leg
forced en to jump ship.

They's both firemen on Titanic
- seems almost funny don't it
now the coal's runnin' low.

This one's my last'un - mind you
I said that last time. Smell the wisps
o' lace-like hair on 'er for'ead. *Ahhh.*

Touch 'er tiny toes, not calloused
like mine! There, there now,
no grislin', Dada home soon.

Fire's burning nice now. See yon piece
glowin' like a demon's eye? Must be
a thousand times that on't ship.

They're good solid lads. They'll see me
right, though I still 'ave that ache
in me breast, like any mother does.

Was that a knock? Don't look
so affeard – news is finally come.
Hold 'er for me, will you dear?

Let us just answer this,
then I'll get us some tea.

Two Captains

(Captain Arthur H Rostron and Captain Stanley T Lord)

Rostron: I was Captain of the rescue ship: *Carpathia*.

Lord: I was Captain of the 'other' ship: *Californian*.

Rostron: We were headed from New York to warmer seas.

Lord: We were packed-in mid-Atlantic by loose ice.

Rostron: We were ready for any ice warnings from nearby ships.

Lord: When we sent an ice warning we were told by Titanic to 'keep out and shut up'.

Rostron: I had just gone to bed when I received news of Titanic's distress call.

Lord: I didn't receive Titanic's distress call.

Rostron: Our Wireless Operator passed the call and coordinates straight to me.

Lord: Our Wireless Operator wasn't operating – he'd turned in for the night.

Rostron: We were fifty-eight miles away.

Lord: We were nineteen miles away.

Rostron: I ordered full steam ahead to our maximum speed.

Lord: I slept soundly, ignorant of Titanic's rockets being fired.

Rostron: I thought of the sea-serpent I once spied off the Irish coast.

Lord: I dreamed of mystery ships steaming away into the night.

Rostron: We arrived as quickly as we could.

Lord: We *could not move* for ice.

Rostron: Closed in...
Lord: Packed-in!
Rostron: ...on the area, careful not to collide with
             the lifeboats, staring in disbelief at the spot
             where she should have been, littered with
             bodies bobbing like dried leaves on the
             surface.
Lord: It is far worse to imagine this scene.
Rostron: We had rooms ready for rescued passengers:
             blankets, hot soup and comforting words.
Lord: As soon as we heard of the sinking, we
             steamed out of the ice, speechless but ready
             to check for bodies.
Rostron: We spent a sombre voyage back to New York.
Lord: We found nothing at the site by the
             coordinates provided.
Rostron: I was awarded a silver Loving Cup and
             medals for all my crew.
Lord: I was preparing myself to be ruined.
Rostron: I was made a hero overnight.
Lord: I was made to suffer as a scapegoat for
             negligence.
Rostron: Every Captain's dream.
Lord: The nightmares will not cease.

Mr J Bruce Ismay

(Chairman of the White Star Line - SAVED)

I believe I articulated my account of proceedings
at the inquiry. I presume your persistence
in pursuing this matter is to uncover some secret
undisclosed. I am afraid I will disappoint you.
Are you acquainted with whom I am? President
of the International Mercantile Marine Company
and Chairman of the White Star Line – inherited
from my honourable father. Are you noting this?
Co-conceiver, with Pirrie, of the concept to construct
three sisters of unrivalled proportions, speed
and luxury. I believe I gave my seed to their creation.
Fathered her across the ocean. Just a passenger.
Did all I could.

I presume your impertinence in uttering her name
in my presence is to provoke some suppressed passion
on my part. Ti...tan...ic. The proper noun has become
abstract, the outline seared in black across my heart.
Lower away! Lower away! Lower indeed, than anyone,
alone in the doctor's room on Carpathia, opiates
warming a laconic smile on my face, as I consoled
my reflection. I regarded myself sideways on
and followed a tear as it traced the jagged line
of my moustache. Like any good father,
I wanted her to achieve great feats.

I believe I did all I could, until it was too late to make
a difference. Of course a representative was required

to present the case to the company: J Bruce Ismay:
'deeply regret ... advise you ... YAMSI': my good name.
No women in sight. Boat half-empty. Took my place.

I presume by your regard that you neglect to condone
my conduct that night. What kind of father would want
to watch his daughter die? What about ... what about ...
the passengers, you say? My deepest condolences
are sent with sincere affection to their loved ones.

Workman at New York Harbour

(20th April 1912)

We were asked to sand her name
off the thirteen recovered lifeboats
and store them in the second floor
loft of piers fifty eight and nine.

As I scraped away at the letters
I tried to make new words
out of them, as Titanic
faded to white.

Annie O'Neill

(Embalmer on the Mackay-Bennett cable ship. 21st April 1912)

I was assigned to the women and children.
Such a sobering sight to see all those coffins
like giant matchboxes stacked up in the hold.

My job is usually performed in isolation.
So many embalmers – everything multiplied
out of any fathomable proportions.

Obviously I have seen dead bodies before
but not in such quantities, and it was hard
to make sense of why some wore pyjamas,

two pairs of trousers, three shirts and an overcoat,
while others were dressed as if about
to step out for a night at the opera.

Some rested peacefully as if merely asleep.
Others had clearly fought with death.
All bobbed upright and expectant in the water.

I wanted to click my fingers and see their eyes
unglaze and colour return to their cheeks
- that is how ready to be rescued they appeared.

I had a procedure to follow. Careful recordings
of hair colour, height, weight, age, any markings
and other physical details. Pockets checked

for jewellery, tickets, passports. All and sundry
were recorded and items placed delicately
into canvas bags, then the bodies were prepared.

One of my first was a boy: blond, 2'1", 37lb,
24 months, little scar above right eyebrow,
in his left pocket a lump of ice still half-frozen.

Gosta Leonard Pålsson. All his family were lost.
In state, for days, he remained at Mayflower
Curling Rink, on ice, unidentified, unclaimed.

Frank Newell

(Undertaker. Nephew of Arthur W Newell - LOST)

Another body, another
list of criteria to check.
Details entered in log.
Bodies everywhere,
alive and dead.

Watching from
the viewing area, framed
in a stricken scene
of expectance: the worst.

Lying prostrate, bloated,
disfigured, broken marble
statues, blue veins of ice.

Another body, another,
this time sickeningly
different - a faintly
familiar face. *Oh God:*
my flesh, my blood,
my uncle.

Claimants

(December 1912)

*I, Mrs Charlotte Cardeza, First Class passenger
claim (amongst other items):*

1 ring, Burmah Ruby and 2 diamonds, Tiffany NY	$14,000
1 chinchilla coat, Irish lace	$ 6,000
1 Lavalliere, platinum chain, canary marquise, white marquise, 22 small diamonds	$ 2,200
1 Baby white lamb coat	$ 1,500
1 iridescent spangled net dress	$ 480
1 music box, little bird	$ 350
1 pink and satin brocade	$ 300
1 Louis Vuitton hat trunk	$ 60
1 light blue velvet hat with pink roses	$ 50

I, Mr Eugene Daly, Third Class passenger claim:

1 set of bagpipes	$ 50

Clock

*(Designed for the carved panel 'Honour and Glory Crowning Time'
at the top of the First Class staircase)*

I was destined to be fitted
into the smooth carved void
beneath Honour and Glory
upon her arrival back to port.

Our union would be the crown
on the head of a successful
maiden voyage.

My intended resting place
rots away,
our delicately crafted marriage
remains
unconsummated.

Arrival

(April 2012. Memory - SAVED)

The scene slips into sepia;
my view like hair-crackled film;
the wind making a hollow sound
like grief when I open my mouth.

The gleaming off-white cruiser
parties past, music blasting,
flaunting its ample bulge of lifeboats;
Caribbean cocktails suspended
casually over the balconies above.

No one's waving. Wave back!

It leaves a yellowy wake-trail
past the end of the dock
and an emptiness of confusion
at something so big being
in place, so rooted, now not.

And there it was: I had it, at least
as much as I could: the experience
of those uninvolved but fascinated
observers who watched her go
just over one hundred years ago.

I follow the trail of her descendant
with my eyes but only some of my heart
which slows to regular pace and the wind

whips under my skirt, rippling it like sails
and everything's played in slow motion.

The liner, nearly gone into a new adventure,
disappears into the brown mist hanging
over the *Test*. The film stops. Silence.
Faces turn back to their cars then leave.

Show's over till next time.

But the film, just a glitch, trip-starts
and I half run, half skip to the end
of the pier. Something propels me
to brace myself to the railings.

It starts as a black line cutting through
the sepia, returning me to colour
when I blink. I see bunting flags
like a dot-to-dot picture steaming ahead,

a determined slice of bow with lines
casting geometrical shapes across the murk,
a white stripe over the top like a smirk,
little square portholes playing tricks on me,
daring me to gasp, and I do.

I see shapes from the past:
handkerchiefs, hats, waving,
clutched by hands on bodies
whose faces I begin to know.

She heads to berth in her old haunt,
and they're back, safe and sound
and swearing over what all the fuss
was about, making me laugh for as long
as it takes her lines to fade out.

S. S. Titanic

*(Steamer Ship, Property of the White Star Line -
LOST and SAVED)*

My berth in Belfast was painful,
suspended in scaffolding, building me
up, out of all proportion. The opposite
of pulling teeth: anchors weighed,
double bottom constructed
('does my bum look big in this?')
Don't laugh. You started this.
I am beyond your wildest dreams.
The Queen of the Ocean. The largest
and most luxurious liner in the world!
Unchristened and heathen, I had
a breech birth out of the gantry,
restrained by anchor chains,
like a circus elephant backing out
of the Big Top wagon. I was guided
to the fitting-out basin for insertion
of triple screws: the penultimate insult.
Finally, the beautification, defining
my features with carved oak panels,
vast domed glass ceilings, gold-plated
chandeliers, white wicker chairs and pure
cotton linen. Tickled, primed and touched-up
with a final lick of black paint; trials passed
and ready for the Maiden Voyage.
The *Virgin*, the *Fallen*, the *Crone*.
Unattainable, unsinkable, (unlikely!)
You raised me to such a height from which

to fall: filled me with the rich and influential,
their wealth and words heavier than me.
Pushed me to the limit; made me fast
and loose at twenty two and a half knots,
sliced me open on the inevitable berg.
Like any good woman I take it all on board.
Feel the cold wet fill my lower compartments.
Release my offspring into the night and split,

falling so low it's taken you nearly a century
to find me. But you'll never really find me.
Though you poke and probe, take samples
of my wrinkled, rusticled form. Never really
understand me. So you'll make me a martyr,
preserve me in relics, raise me up even higher
than before. My maker, my keeper, my enemy.

Bibliography

Beesley, L (1912) *The Loss of the S.S. Titanic.* New York: Houghton Mifflin Co.

Braynard, F (1988) *Story of the Titanic.* USA: Dover Publications.

Eaton, J P & Haas, C (1986) *Titanic – Triumph and Tragedy.* Somerset: Patrick Stephens Ltd.

Gracie, Col. A (2008) *Titanic – A Survivor's Story.* Gloucestershire: The History Press.

Hirst, H (2010) *Titanic Pocket Series.* Wiltshire: Instinctive Product Development.

Hyslop, D et al (2006) *Titanic Voices.* Southampton: Southampton City Council.

Layton, J K (2004) *Atlantic Liners* – Mysteries – Music to Drown By. www.atlanticliners.com

Lord, W (1976) *A Night to Remember.* London: Penguin Books.

Lynch, D & Marschall, K (2003) *Ghosts of the Abyss.* Ontario: Madison Press Books.

Maltin, T & Aston, E (2010) *101 Things you Thought you Knew about the Titanic but Didn't.* London: Beautiful Books.

Marcus, G (1969) *The Maiden Voyage.* London: George Allen & Unwin Ltd.

Marschall, K & Lynch, D (1992) *Titanic - An Illustrated History.* London: Hodder & Stoughton.

Matsen, B (2008) *Titanic's Last Secrets.* New York: Twelve.

Matthews, R (2011) *Titanic – The Tragic Story of the Ill-Fated Ocean Liner.* London: Arcturus Publishing Ltd.

Maxtone-Graham, J (2010) *Titanic Survivor: The Memoirs of Violet Jessop - Stewardess.* Gloucestershire: The History Press.

Riffenburgh, B (2008) *The Titanic Experience.* London: Sevenoaks Publishing.

Robertson, M (1898) *Futility – The Wreck of the Titan.* USA: Buccaneer Books.

Stringer, C (2002) *Titanic People*. UK: Family History Indexes.

Turner, S (2011) *The Band that Played On*. USA: Thomas Nelson.

White, E E (1998) *Voyage on the Great Titanic: The Diary of Margaret Anne Brady 1912*. London: Scholastic.

Titanic Replica Pack. Edinburgh: Memorabilia Pack Company.